Making Bar Graphs

By Jagger Youssef

Gareth Stevens
PUBLISHING

[leveled
reader]
math

Please visit our website, www.garethstevens.com. For a free color catalog of all our high-quality books, call toll free 1-800-542-2595 or fax 1-877-542-2596.

Library of Congress Cataloging-in-Publication Data

Youssef, Jagger.
Making bar graphs / by Jagger Youssef.
    p. cm. — (Graph it!)
Includes index.
ISBN 978-1-4824-0782-2 (pbk.)
ISBN 978-1-4824-0828-7 (6-pack)
ISBN 978-1-4824-0779-2 (library binding)
1. Graphic methods — Juvenile literature. 2. Mathematics — Charts, diagrams, etc. — Juvenile literature. 3. Mathematical statistics — Graphic methods — Juvenile literature. I. Title.
QA40.5 Y68 2015
510—d23

Published in 2015 by
Gareth Stevens Publishing
111 East 14th Street, Suite 349
New York, NY 10003

Designer: Katelyn E. Reynolds
Editor: Therese Shea

Photo credits: Cover, pp. 1–24 (background texture) ctrlaplus/Shutterstock.com; cover, pp. 1, 7, 9, 11, 13, 17, 19, 21 (bar graph elements) Colorlife/Shutterstock.com; p. 5 Valter Dias/Shutterstock.com; p. 17 (photo) Tyler Olson/Shutterstock.com.

Printed in the United States of America

CPSIA compliance information: Batch #CS15GS: For further information contact Gareth Stevens, New York, New York at 1-800-542-2595.

Contents

Boldface words appear in the glossary.

Get into Graphs

Graphs help us count and **compare**. There are many kinds of graphs. A bar graph uses bars, or rectangles, that stand for numbers. Bar graphs are a fun way to show facts!

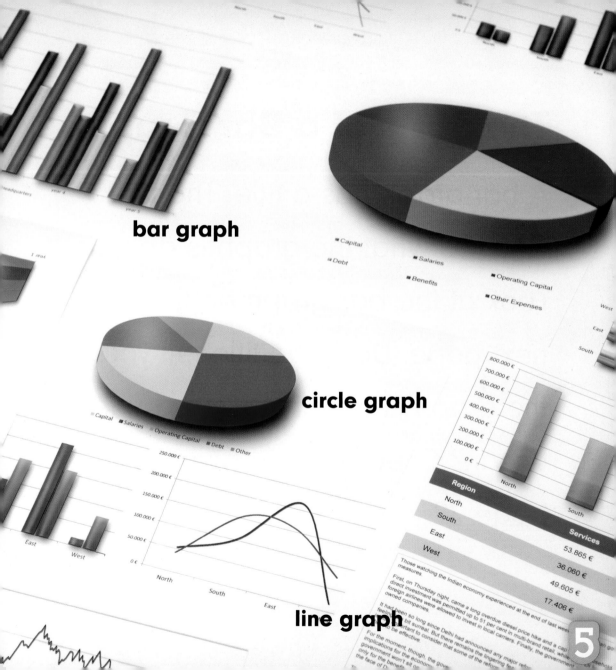

bar graph

circle graph

line graph

5

The Parts of a Bar Graph

A bar graph has a title. The title tells you what the graph is about. Look at the bar graph on the next page. Does the title tell you the graph is about the zoo or the ocean? Check your answer on page 22.

Who's at the Zoo?

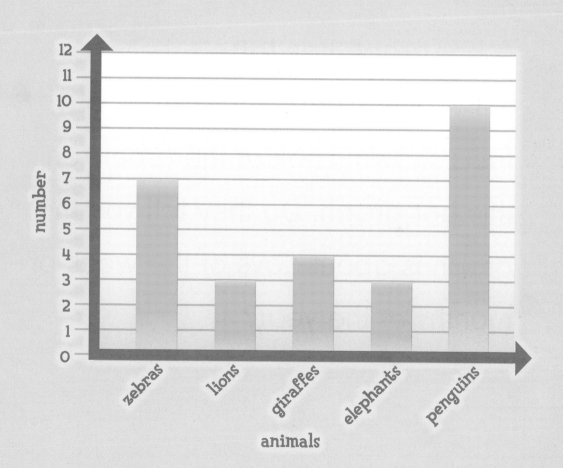

A bar graph has **labels**. Labels tell you more about the kinds of facts shown. Look at the labels on this bar graph. Do they tell you the graph is about days of the week or months of the year?

A Rainy Spring

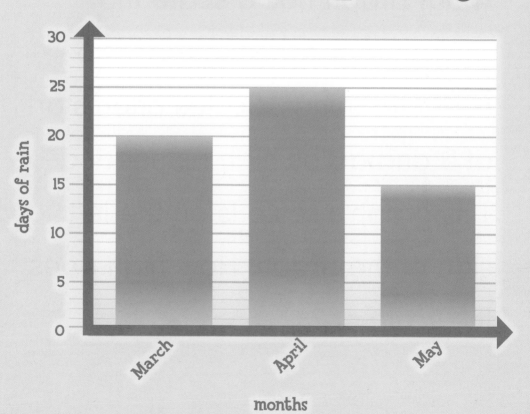

A bar graph has a **scale** that shows the numbers needed to compare things. Scales often start at 0 and go as high as needed. This graph's scale is on the left side of the graph. How high does the scale go?

Favorite Field Trips

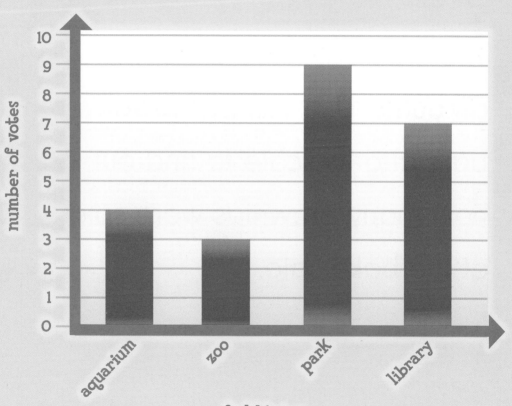

The bars on a bar graph tell you amounts. Use this bar graph's bars and its scale to find out how many brownies were sold at the bake sale.

Bake Sale

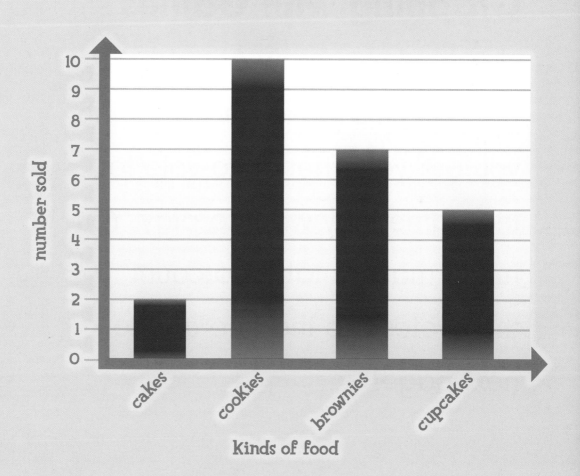

Graphing with Games

Now that you know about bar graphs, let's make one. Imagine you ask your friends to vote for the game they want to play. You might make a table to count their votes like the one on the next page.

kinds of games	number of votes
Frisbee	3
checkers	2
soccer	5

Now turn your table into a bar graph. Draw it on a piece of paper. Your labels should be "kinds of games" and "number of votes." Your scale needs to include the largest number of votes, 5. Draw lines going across the graph.

number of votes

5
4
3
2
1
0

kinds of games

Now put the bars into your bar graph. Make sure each bar goes up to the correct number of votes. Label each. Finally, include a title, such as "What Should We Play?" According to your graph, which game won the vote?

What Should We Play?

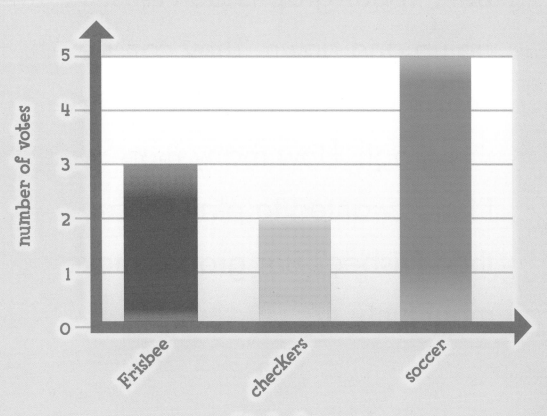

Bars in bar graphs don't just go up and down. They can be shown from left to right, like in this graph. How many more friends wanted to play soccer than Frisbee? Bar graphs make math fun!

What Should We Play?

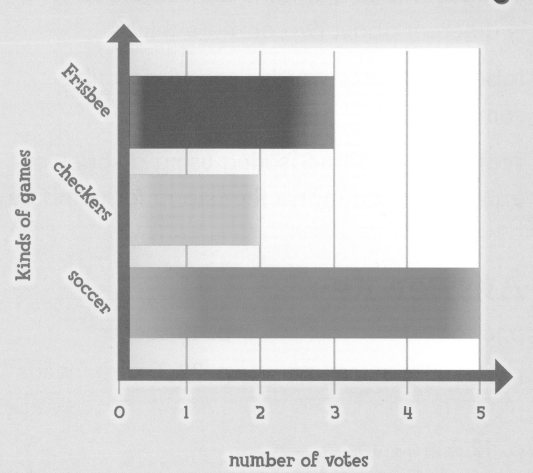

number of votes

Glossary

compare: to find what is the same and what is different about two or more things

label: a word or words used to describe something

scale: a way of measuring using a series of equally spaced marks that stand for numbers

Answer Key

p. 6 zoo

p. 8 months of the year

p. 10 10

p. 12 7 brownies

p. 18 soccer

p. 20 2 more friends

For More Information

Books

Bodach, Vijaya. *Bar Graphs*. Mankato, MN: Capstone Press, 2008.

Nelson, Robin. *Let's Make a Bar Graph*. Minneapolis, MN: Lerner Publications, 2013.

Websites

Bar Graphs
www.mathsisfun.com/data/bar-graphs.html
Learn how a table can be turned into a bar graph.

Interpret Bar Graphs
www.ixl.com/math/grade-2/interpret-bar-graphs
Practice answering questions using bar graphs.

Tally Charts and Bar Graphs
www.brainpopjr.com/math/data/tallychartsandbargraphs/
Watch a video to learn about two kinds of graphs.

Publisher's note to educators and parents: Our editors have carefully reviewed these websites to ensure that they are suitable for students. Many websites change frequently, however, and we cannot guarantee that a site's future contents will continue to meet our high standards of quality and educational value. Be advised that students should be closely supervised whenever they access the Internet.

Index